Why Is The Economy Like This?!

Why Is The Economy Like This?!

Cornelis Bal

Copyright © 2014 by Cornelis Bal.

Library of Congress Control Number   2014920145
ISBN: Hardcover   978-1-4990-9178-6
             Softcover   978-1-4990-9177-9
             eBook   978-1-4990-9176-2

All rights reserved. No part of this book may be reproduced or transmitted in any form or by any means, electronic or mechanical, including photocopying, recording, or by any information storage and retrieval system, without permission in writing from the copyright owner.

Any people depicted in stock imagery provided by Thinkstock are models, and such images are being used for illustrative purposes only.
Certain stock imagery © Thinkstock.

This book was printed in the United States of America.

Rev. date: 11/07/2014

To order additional copies of this book, contact:
Xlibris
0-800-056-3182
www.xlibrispublishing.co.uk
Orders@xlibrispublishing.co.uk
697955

Contents

Preface 7

Chapter 1
Introduction 9

Chapter 2
The law of economics 21

Chapter 3
Analysis and prediction 35

Chapter 4
Solution 41

Preface

This book is about:

- how the present worldwide economic laws and regulations rule and influence our lives
- wondering, why is it like this?
- making some suggestions on how we could go about changing the present economic system
- suggesting a possible alternative system.

If you are looking for any calculative justifications for the statements in this book, do not read this book (the people who claim being able to make these calculative justifications have a vested interest in proving that the analysis is wrong and that the suggestions are rubbish).

CORNELIS BAL

Whatever is stated in this book is based on common sense.

It is from accumulated knowledge and from other people who do know!

Proving that you are right makes you uncertain. My father used to say. You don't have to pick up dog shit to know that it stinks.

Another person in my life I wish to mention is my wife, Susan.

In spite of me boring her with my repetitive (and very, very boring) stories, she still loves me, and I love her more than anything else in this world.

I wish to thank and acknowledge all people (through publications, discussions, etc.) from whom I have accumulated the wisdom (or what some might call stupidity) expressed in this book.

Chapter 1

Introduction

This book is about the way in which we have organized our society in today's world.

People working in the commercial sector of the economy generate money. This money is creamed off by tax. Government uses this money to cover their expenses including support for the unemployed.

All of us like freedom. Freedom is not a "Do what you want freedom". It is freedom within a system, and we accept that. Believers in total freedom do also stop at red traffic lights.

Have you ever wondered how much freedom is taken from us by the way in which we have arranged our economic system?

We will get to that further on.

Old sayings like the following have a direct effect on (immediate after you are born):

- Money is everything.
- If you are born for a dime, you will never be a quarter (translated from Dutch and is probably lost in translation for many readers).
- It is not affordable! (This is a very popular saying by governments.)
- The list is soooo long.

The saying 'We have to work for a living' indicates how important (paid) jobs are to us, but does the present system create enough opportunities to actually do that?

Before we get into that, let us see the two aspects that have a major impact on our lives:

- laws of nature
- law of economics.

WHY IS THE ECONOMY LIKE THIS?!

The laws of nature make us build things and use them.

We can build aeroplanes, motor cars, and ships, and we can use electricity. For all these, we use the laws of nature.

We live comfortably in cold countries by using heating and air conditioning in hot countries.

We can build high and spanning structures.

We (most of us) can swim, and that is probably one of best examples of using the laws of nature.

We can launch into and keep things in space.

We can build computers and connect them through waves (Wi-Fi).

We can watch television and listen to the radio. Whoever does that any more?

We can cure illnesses of which the existence was unknown ten years ago.

We can even produce body parts so that we can soon stop stealing them from (fresh!) dead bodies.

We can build weapons that can hit people on the other side of the world without exposing ourselves (some consider that very useful).

All these things are designed and built based on the laws of nature.

The laws of nature are very precise and very dependable (and we should be grateful for it).

There are still a lot of unknown laws of nature. We call them mysteries, but they are not mysteries. We are simply not clever enough yet to figure them out, or we face multiple laws of nature acting together and have not yet fully worked out the interactive ratio. In conclusion, nature is beautiful.

- We can trust the laws of nature as they are 100 per cent repetitive.

WHY IS THE ECONOMY LIKE THIS?!

- Laws of nature also have an accumulative aspect, which is called evolution!
- We learn how to use the laws of nature at an increasing rate.
- Figuring out the laws of nature will help us to live longer and have an easier life.

But we take the laws of nature for granted more than often.

We do not always realize how helpless we would be if any of these laws would stop to exist, like if the sun would be switched off.

With regards to nature's evolution; development of discovery, implementation, and using the laws of nature follows a progressive curve.

The difference between life 50 years ago and now is much more different than life between 500 years ago until 50 years ago.

If I had told my grandfather fifty years ago that I would be able to speak to somebody on the other side of the globe using a device as small as his tobacco package (yes, he did roll his own cigarettes), he would have recommended to my father to have me locked up in an institution.

While we could not look fifty years ahead then, we cannot even look five years ahead now.

Companies used to make yearly budgets and stick to them until the year was over.

Companies now make quarterly rolling budgets, review, and adjust quarterly.

Long-term plans meant twenty years long then but now we have difficulty looking reliably two years ahead.

The telex machine was around for 100 years and peaked at 1.2 million machines in the world. It was replaced by the fax machine and there were 1.2 million fax machines operating within 2 years, but who uses fax now?

WHY IS THE ECONOMY LIKE THIS?!

The life cycle of products is reduced to such a level that IT products must deliver a profit within two years or the products are considered a commercial failure.

Schools churn out students for jobs that do not exist yet.

In the graph depicting this progressive curve, the line between 500 years ago until 50 years ago is almost horizontal while it is almost vertical now!

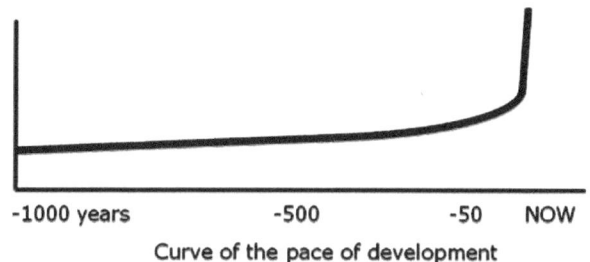

Curve of the pace of development

That does not seem to make us very much smarter when it comes to managing our resources.

For example, we take some resources from the environment at a much higher rate than nature can reproduce them.

We dig into the capital rather than living off the interest.

We do that by using fossil fuels. In fact, there is plenty of energy around, and we are capable of tapping into it.

We do not have an energy shortage; we just have no means of storing energy and using it where and when it is needed. We have just not yet designed a box in which we can store it so that we can use it when and where required.

The best idea that we have come up so far is storing a small amount of energy in a battery.

Some people have estimated that 70 per cent of the energy is lost in transmission. Trucks use up to 80 per cent of their fuel to power the truck and only 20 per cent to carry the load. We can move goods through pipelines more cheaply and more effectively.

WHY IS THE ECONOMY LIKE THIS?!

Yes, *nature* is one of my favourite words, and the 'green' people are right in many ways although they are not always presenting their case comprehensively.

Nature also generates accumulation of knowledge over time (popularly known as evolution), which also proves that whatever brilliant idea we come up with, it is always thanks to what other people have done before.

More interesting chapters can be written about the way the laws of nature are used in our society, but this book is more about the law of economics.

This law of economics is the other aspect that has a major impact on our lives too, but it is not as predictable and reliable as the laws of nature.

It causes havoc more than often.

The economic laws are made by a relatively small number of people that have (and had) both the power and a selfish interest in creating the rules and regulations as we know them now.

We seem to be stuck with these rules and regulations to such an extent that we are reluctant to even believe that we can change them.

First conclusion:

Laws of nature apply to all people indiscriminately while the law of economics seems to favour a limited number of people only.

WHY IS THE ECONOMY LIKE THIS?!

First question of

'Why is the economy like this?'

is

'Why do we continue to accept
the implementation of these
rules and regulations?'

Chapter 2

The law of economics

I want you to know that I am not a socialist! I am a realist.

The law of economics seems to concentrate on developing business in the hope that people will benefit. It has led to a global society which favours a limited number of people over others.

Yes, I know it still sounds very socialistic, but keep on reading (if you have the guts).

We basically have two economic systems:

- capitalism
- communism.

When the Soviet Union broke up and the influence of communism was 'lessening' (new word) in other communistic-type countries, some people were of the opinion that the capitalistic system had won.

It certainly seemed to look that way initially, but now there are strong signs that capitalism is about to fail too.

Let me first try to explain why I believe that communism had no future from the beginning.

The two basic features which we cannot change—as if they are embedded in our DNA—are:

- jealousy/envy
- greed.

These features are definitely present in all of us although they may manifest differently from individual to individual.

They influence us both in the way we feel as well as in the way we act. That may be very different from situation to situation.

WHY IS THE ECONOMY LIKE THIS?!

Whatever system we come up with, it has to consider that.

Let me try to explain with an example how this affects us and makes us act differently.

You have dinner, and you share a table with two strangers. Out of the blue, one of them gives you a crisp, new $100 bill. That makes you feel good, and you like that person while you have no particular opinion about the other person at the table.

Then the $100 person turns to the other guy and gives him two crisp $100 bills.

Nobody took anything from you, but you no longer feel good, and you now have a very peculiar feeling about the guy US $200 richer.

This is jealousy/envy and greed working in you at record levels.

You are ready to question the actions of the guy who gave you a $100 bill in spite of the fact that he has treated you generously.

CORNELIS BAL

Communism tried to let you suppress the embedded aspects of jealousy/envy and greed and tried to interest you as an individual to work for a greater cause.

It does *not* work.

We are unique individuals, and we do not want to be considered equal to others.

We are proud of our achievements, and we want to be recognized and rewarded appropriately.

We want to be treated equally, but that is different from being equal.

Capitalism recognizes that and rewards that too.

It works very, very well as long as we have 85 people and 100 jobs.

When there are 100 people and 85 jobs, it does not work so well.

WHY IS THE ECONOMY LIKE THIS?!

The fact is that the economy is growing but lesser and lesser people are involved in it. This is mainly a result from technological developments.

Paid jobs are disappearing, and the level of joblessness (the lack of paid jobs) will continue to increase.

You can argue against that until you are blue in the face, but

It is a fact

More and more things can be made by machines (robots), and these machines can carry out service-type tasks too.

Applying these machines is no longer limited to high-tech producers only.

Machines produce stuff at 'lower than present' costs and at good quality too while manual jobs disappear like snow to the sun—and that applies to services too.

Hardly anyone processes your boarding pass or your passport to get on board an aeroplane, and that is just an example.

- You put a piece of plastic into a machine, and you have your boarding pass.
- You stick your finger into another machine or look into a little hole, and you have passed immigration.

For producing products, it is so much easier to get into any business as machines have the production skills, and soon these skills are given to machines by other machines.

This accelerates the shifting of location of jobs. What was traditionally a local product (Dutch cheese, Parma ham, etc.) can now be produced anywhere with machines.

WHY IS THE ECONOMY LIKE THIS?!

The owner of the machines does not have to have any specific skills other than good taste and clever marketing.

There is also the issue of the way and speed that developing countries are catching up with developed countries.

After the World War II, a lot of jobs went to Japan. They produced at low price but copied products until the manpower costs levelled with the West, and the jobs went elsewhere.

Japan now produces high-quality products, and the 'elsewhere people' do copy them now.

It took Japan thirty years; it will take the 'elsewhere people' three years to reach that level of no longer copying existing designs.

Germany is now the number one exporter, but very soon their products will be copied and produced cheaply but at similar quality (yes, good quality can be achieved by the machines as they no longer depend on manual skills).

When Japan got into the act, the 'producing' world had 500 million people involved in it, and Japan 60 million people. Today's producing world has 1 billion people, but other countries (India, China, Indonesia, and some smaller countries) are trying to get into the act, and they have a combined total of 2.5 billion people.

Considering the advanced technology, it is unimaginable what effect that will have on the world economy in its present form.

The number of A grade students in India is higher then the total number of students in the USA.

These statistics will have an (unpredictable) effect on our future.

History repeats itself, but at a much faster pace.

WHY IS THE ECONOMY LIKE THIS?!

Present efforts to try to prevent the jobs going to low-labour-cost countries or to robots can be compared with trying to

treat cancer with Band-Aid.

To be absolutely correct, the issue is no longer simply about low-cost countries.

The issue is much more complex due to technological developments, number of people, and a much faster catch-up phase than in the past.

In the years of ninety sixty, my family had one bicycle, but an American family had three cars.

Now, I do not have a tablet, but most sons of farmers in developing countries do have one.

It shows that the difference between developed and developing countries is different from what it used to be.

Disappearing jobs is a fact of life in today's world, and it has (will have) a devastating effect on our lives, so we better focus on how to deal with it quickly.

The emphasis of the above statement is on the way that we have organized ourselves economically.

Some people may argue that perhaps, besides the influence of nature and economics, the type of government is also a major influencing factor. I disagree with it; whatever the government format is in place, the language is all the same when it comes to taking labour decisions—it depends on whether it is affordable.

- Do we implement health care for the people?
    - We can't afford it.

WHY IS THE ECONOMY LIKE THIS?!

- Do we go green?
    - We can't afford it.

- Do we have a pension?
    - We can't afford it.

- Do we build high-speed train services?
    - We can't afford it.

So we are back to the two major aspects that influence our daily live (laws of nature and the law of economics). The impact from the type of regime is much smaller.

The Arab Spring was not about regime; it was about jobs (or more precisely, the lack of jobs) and about having your back against the wall without being able to yield any further.

The Middle East population had exploded in the last thirty years at a 25 per cent yearly rate, and there were no jobs to fill that kind of manpower increase.

This 'spring' thing started in Tunisia, North Africa; a university graduate who could not find a job had to resort to selling fruits, for which he had no licence, and a (lady) government agent pushed him over the edge.

He had no safety net, and being desperate, he killed himself publicly. He set himself on fire in front of the city hall.

That desperate act was recognized by many, and it led to a countrywide uprising.

It went over the borders into Egypt and other Middle Eastern countries.

It had little to do with the government although there was the influence of country density.

Lesser-density (and smaller) countries were less affected as they seemed to be more manageable.

WHY IS THE ECONOMY LIKE THIS?!

If you live outside the Middle East, do not think that your country is safe from a 'spring' wave.

Spain and Greece had a taste of it for exactly the same reason—no jobs.

If there are jobs or there is a safety net (unemployment benefits), it is manageable.

Chapter 3
Analysis and prediction

In our present economic system, the number of paid jobs is diminishing (please remember that this economic system is man-made and we *can* change it).

The ratio of unpaid people will increase.

In the present system, the paid people will somehow pay for a society that supports the unpaid people.

It is a matter of fact, and the people with the jobs cannot kill the unpaid people or send them to another planet. (For some people, this idea sounds tempting, but it is a definite *no-no!*)

Increasingly, there will be growing resistance of the paying people as their spendable income will decrease due to the fact that their portion of income to support the unpaid people will steadily increase.

It will ultimately create a two-grade society:

- Grade 1 - the people that hold paid jobs
- Grade 2 - the people that do not hold paid jobs.

The grade 2 people will have a different composition from the present jobless people.

The present jobless people are mainly the low-educated people (they do not have a united voice although they have the numbers), but that will change.

This new generation of well-educated but unpaid job holders will probably organize themselves better, and within our democratic system, they will form a powerful group obsessed with one objective only.

Anarchy may very well be on the horizon.

It flares up occasionally; the moment injustice is done in the eyes of the jobless, there will be an outbreak of self-service shopping, which is done without stopping at the cash register (rioting).

Another disturbing factor is that the banks force themselves on us via never-ending advertising campaigns, but they have no real function in our system.

They know that, which is why they have to spend all this advertising money to convince us.

They do not contribute to society, but they take a cut from every transaction that is done from both the people with paid jobs as well as the people with unpaid jobs, and they give hardly anything back.

CORNELIS BAL

In 2013 one of the banks announced profits of multibillion US dollars while, on the same page of the newspaper, indicated that they were planning to reduce their workforce by 3,000.

Charity is also hiding a few aspects in our present economic achievements, and some states already try to calculate the economic volume of charity so that it can be included into the economic achievement.

All in all, it is my opinion that the present economic system should be changed, and it shall adopt the latest technological developments.

Why do we see so much technological developments but the political picture has not changed in 200 years?

The people in Great Britain have decided 200 years ago that the 'one man equals one vote' is applicable, but they still hang on to the House of Lords.

This house is filled with people on the basis of their so-called birthright.

The politicians seem to be more interested in re-election than they are in government.

Government is supposed to lead us into the future, but why is it that most governments still live in the past?

If we want a sustainable future for ourselves, we need to start acting fast.

We have to make changes that are in tune with today's technology.

Chapter 4
Solution

I wish I could leave this chapter empty because I feel that although I am reasonably good at analysing the present situation, it is so much more difficult to come up with a solution for a new system.

In the eyes of many people, that disqualifies me from commenting on the present system.

To my defence, our present system was built up over hundreds of years, and it was created bit by bit by many very clever people, and having one person to come up with a new system that solves all is a bit too much to ask.

CORNELIS BAL

I can express my opinion about what could be some of the basics for a new system, but the new system (if that is what we want) should be formed from the collective input of all people.

I will not accept the old-fashioned opinion that

they do not know what they want!

That worked for ages in the old world, but that time has passed.

It is the duty of today's governments to inform the people about the options and organize expressions of opinions and act accordingly.

This is my message to governments:

> We people are not really as stupid as you would like us to be.

WHY IS THE ECONOMY LIKE THIS?!

We could organize a worldwide discussion, preceded by sharing educational information (when I say educational information, I mean just that, and it should not be confused with indoctrination/propaganda).

We could get some of the smartest people to write about it and express their opinion, but let the masses decide.

Earlier in this book, I stated:

> The law of economics seems to concentrate on developing business, hoping that people will benefit.

Now I'd like to state:

> Let us concentrate on people, and business will benefit.

The new system could consider paying people for their contribution to society instead of just paying them for their contribution to the economic system.

That would include a lot more people (if not all) into the economic system.

In discussions on this subject, I would ask, which people do contribute to society tremendously but do not get paid?

I have yet to get the right answer.

The answer is *mothers*.

Without them,

    we would not even be here!

They represent about 50 per cent of the world population!

They spent their lives shaping and forming the people on this planet.

Ignoring groups in our society will lead to anarchy sooner or later.

WHY IS THE ECONOMY LIKE THIS?!

Are we going to wait until that happens (and it will happen) and deal with it in a reactive manner, or are we going to prove that we did learn from history and be pro-active?

We are smarter now.

We are getting smarter faster.

Are we going to continue to be concentrating on (distracted by) details like emerging markets (Chinese, Indian, Indonesian, etc.) and robots taking our jobs, or are we going to prepare ourselves for the future that has been brought to our doorstep?

So let us try to design a system that has natural features (accumulative and evolutionary).

Our present system lacks these features. It does not accumulate and is not evolutionary.

CORNELIS BAL

It creates groups in our society, and as such, it divides.

In the animal world, many predators work together to survive—killer whales, lions, hyenas, etc.

It is through evolution that they have developed that survival skill by cooperation, and they will survive (if human beings don't interfere).

Although they are aggressive animals towards their prey, they live together in harmony.

Let us try to learn from that and come up with a system in which every human being has a value at birth; it can grow (or reduce) depending on what that human being does with that life.

It can be expressed in a value that is electronically controlled and from which that person can arrange its life.

WHY IS THE ECONOMY LIKE THIS?!

The value can increase (or decrease) depending on the contribution that this person brings to society.

The contribution to society should be the cornerstone to evolution.

It can turn us away from the present destructive path.

Many things are considered as required in our society, but as we have determined that we cannot afford them, some of these things are now done by volunteers and are supported by charity.

This makes that type of work very dependable, for which people should be grateful.

For what?

Did they put themselves into that situation of requiring help?

CORNELIS BAL

Most of the time, *no*.

They did not ask for the tsunami, cyclone, typhoon, excessive rainy/dry weather, earthquake, disability, having cancer at being eight years old only, unemployment, Ebola epidemic, etc.

So there is a lot of (manual) work to be done that is now not possible because we seemingly cannot afford it!

There are a lot of differences in the world in terms of development, and we all know that the levelling process cannot be stopped; why fight it?

There has been a long traditional fight between the conservative and progressive people about accepting new things.

This put the brakes on development.

It is really a waste of effort as it usually ends up with

WHY IS THE ECONOMY LIKE THIS?!

when it will be accepted

rather than

whether it will be accepted.

The difference between conservative and progressive people can be described as fifteen years.

Some advanced countries consider the advancement of other countries threatening.

These other countries will advance too.

There is no stopping it, and it will happen.

Any attempts to slow down its pace will only result in unnecessary tension.

Nature develops in an evolution type of manner by going from single-cell life forms into complex, brainy human beings.

It is a constantly advancing process.

CORNELIS BAL

Let us learn from nature, put our heads together, and come up with a system that aims at using developments in an evolutionary type of manner.

It is about time that we learn how to live together by using each other's strength to survive.

We have seen nations rise and fall in history. We all agree that it happened due to one nation overpowering other nations. This is then followed by other nations growing stronger, causing the fall of the conquerors.

> We (humans) do not accept being used/controlled by others.

With the exception of some areas, we no longer have this overwhelming military dominance in today's world.

But we do seem to have developed a different type of dominance.

WHY IS THE ECONOMY LIKE THIS?!

There is a diminishing proportion of working people relative to the non-working people

Ultimately, this will disrupt society.

We are on the way to self-destruction.

We use money as one of the things that separates us from the rest of the creatures in nature. (One of the other things that separate us from the rest of other creatures is our ability to communicate in writing).

It is the way that we put money to use (misuse) that leads to ultimate failure.

We invented paper money, which was originally only worth something if it was backed up with a valuable.

For a long time, that was gold.

We have already done away with most of the gold reserves, which is a step in the right direction.

CORNELIS BAL

Let us find a way to make the next step; it will not be easy, but let us rise up to the challenge.

It was only fifty years ago that we barely knew about computers, let alone what kind of development that could bring us.

The way our system uses money now divides people between:

- the people that have it and the people that do not have it

- the people that can 'make' money and the people that can't 'make' money.

We can consider an economic system which values

contribution to society.

WHY IS THE ECONOMY LIKE THIS?!

In this way, all people are included in the economic system.

The difficulty, I suppose, is how we can organize it so that this contribution to society can be valued and traded.

> Considering all our other achievements, this should not be a very hard nut to crack.

The 'it is considered impossible' argument is no valid excuse for not trying.

Many things which could not even be imagined possible can now be done, and these things had a much lesser impact on our daily lives.

We can imagine this different approach, so it can be done.

The implication of the presently uneven playing field of developed and developing countries is probably one of the biggest obstacles.

CORNELIS BAL

The introduction of a new system that includes all seems to have a better future than continuing trying to patch the existing system which divides people.

I wish to end with a final remark.

We have agreed on a human rights rule, but it may be time to have a 'human sense of duty' rule too.

The human rights rule stipulates

    society's obligation to you.

The 'human sense of duty' rule could stipulate

    your obligation to society.

www.ingramcontent.com/pod-product-compliance
Lightning Source LLC
Chambersburg PA
CBHW021044180526
45163CB00005B/2272